Map of the

A play

William Nicholson

Samuel French - London
New York - Toronto - Hollywood

MAP OF THE HEART

First produced at the Yvonne Arnaud Theatre, February 13th, 1991, and subsequently at the Globe Theatre with the following cast of characters:

Ruth Steadman	Sinead Cusack
Albie Steadman	Patrick Malahide
Sally Steadman	Imogen Boorman
Bernard Fisher	David Rintoul
Angus Ross	Jack Klaff
Mary Hanlon	Susan Wooldridge
Andrew Rainer	Frederick Treves
Smithy	Timothy Page
June Armitage	Tacye Nichols

Directed by Peter Wood
Designed by Mark Thompson

Also published by Samuel French Ltd:

Shadowlands by William Nicholson

ACT I

When the CURTAIN *rises the stage is dark*

An organ plays the introduction to the communion anthem, "Panis Angelicus"

The Lights come up on Ruth Steadman, who stands facing the audience in a part of the stage which represents the choir loft in a church. Ruth is in her forties; an attractive woman who thinks little of her looks

The introduction ends, and Ruth starts to sing. She sings simply and well, but she is not a trained singer. She makes almost no physical movements as she sings, and no effort shows on her face, yet everything in her being is clearly surrendering to the song that pours from her

Ruth   "Panis angelicus
              Fit panis hominum . . ."

As the anthem ends

   Ruth exits

The Lights come up on the living-room of the Steadman home. Sunday morning. Present time

The room is an island of security within a great empty space: suggestions of fortress and prison, as well as that supreme object of desire, the English country home. This house is Ruth's creation, and the sustaining of it has become her purpose in life

The endless space beyond the room, seen through tall windows, is also a view of open country; considered the glory of the house. There are two doors; one to the kitchen and one to the hall

There is a piano, with framed family photographs standing on it and a piano stool. There is a fireplace, in which a fire is dying. By the fire there is a poker, some logs and an ottoman with a Sunday newspaper and colour supplement on it

There is a drinks cabinet complete with glasses and bottles of alcohol, with a telephone on it. Ruth's desk is in front of a window, which has a lamp on it and a make-up bag inside. There is also a sofa and several easy chairs

   Albie Steadman stands with his back to the audience, looking out at the view. He is in his mid-forties, but looks older; one of those people who settle early into middle age and are at home in it. He turns and begins to speak to an imaginary audience, pacing back and forth as he speaks, rehearsing a speech he is due to make later

Albie I'd like to tell you a story. It's about a boy who stayed at home, and always did his homework. Let's call him Albie. Now little Albie had a secret. Albie's secret was that, contrary to appearances, he didn't want to stay at home at all. He wanted to be—an explorer. (*His pacing has brought him before the tall windows. He stops and studies the view*) He wants to go south. Down the river to the sea. Across France, across Spain, to Africa.

Sally Steadman enters, as Albie is speaking. She is seventeen years old, pretty, with a mass of long hair that makes her look young for her age. She has just got out of bed, and is not yet dressed for the day. She has come to purloin a Sunday paper

Africa is a long, long way from home.
Sally Who are you talking to, Dad?
Albie Myself.
Sally You can't have been. You were talking aloud.
Albie If you must know, I was trying out an idea for my speech, at my farewell dinner. Have you just got out of bed?
Sally Yes.
Albie You know it's nearly lunchtime?
Sally (*looking for the colour supplement*) It's a bit dodgy, talking to yourself.
Albie It's not dodgy at all. Try it. Think something, then say it aloud.
Sally You'd hear me.
Albie I won't listen. (*He puts his fingers in his ears and makes a buzzing noise so that he can't hear*)
Sally (*thinking her thought and then speaking it aloud*) I wish Dad wouldn't go to Africa.
Albie (*unplugging his ears*) Well?
Sally Did you hear?
Albie No. I was buzzing.

There is the sound of the front door opening and closing off-stage. Ruth and Bernard are heard entering

Sally starts to beat a hasty retreat

So what did you say?
Sally Doesn't matter. I'm not up yet, okay?

Sally exits

Albie picks up the newspaper and starts to read it

Ruth enters, returning from church, followed by Bernard Fisher, her elder brother. They are laughing and arguing about a half-forgotten verse from a music hall song

Ruth Can't.
Bernard Can.

Ruth Bet?

Bernard Fiver. (*He starts to play the tune on the piano, recalling the words as he goes along*)

(*Singing*)	"Mabel the fair pulled out my hair
	And clawed all the skin off my nose."
	So unsqueamish.
	"She was a dear little dicky bird—"
Ruth (*singing*)	"Cheep, cheep, cheep, she went—"
Bernard	"Sweet-ly she sang to me
	Till all my money was spent.
	Then she stopped her song—"
Ruth	"*Went off* song—"
Bernard	"We parted on fighting terms—"
Ruth } (*together*)	"She was one of the early birds,
Bernard }	And I was one of the worms."

Ruth looks in her purse, to pay her bet

Albie already has a five-pound note waiting. She takes it from him and gives it to Bernard

Bernard Thank you.

Ruth Only just. Oh, Albie, you've let the fire go out.

Albie Have I? Are you sure it's out? Hallo, Bernard.

Bernard Good-morning, Albie.

Ruth How can you not notice? (*She moves to the fireplace*)

Albie I'll deal with it.

But Ruth is already at the fireplace, as he knew she would be

Ruth No, get Bernard a drink. Your fires always go out.

Bernard has not waited to be asked, and is already making himself a drink

Albie Vodka for Bernard.

Bernard Thank you, Albie. Roo and I have much to be thankful for, you know. While all the other children were singing "She loves you, yeah, yeah, yeah", we were singing "Mabel the fair pulled out my hair." It gives one an entirely distinctive outlook on life.

Albie feels guilty about the way Ruth is having to labour at the fire

Albie I really don't know why we don't get one of those instant gas-log fires. I can never tell the difference.

Ruth Oh, Albie. That's like planting the garden with artificial flowers.

Albie Well. It would be less work.

Ruth restarts the fire. She rises and heads for the kitchen

Ruth Did you baste the lamb?

It is clear from Albie's face that he has forgotten

Oh, Albie!

Ruth exits

Albie What's your position on labour-saving fires, Bernard? (*He pours himself a drink*)

Bernard Oh, I'm very down on labour-saving. Labour-evading, now, that's something else. I warm myself at other people's fires. (*He drinks*)

Albie Cheers.

Bernard Cheers.

Albie So how was church? Did Ruth sing?

Bernard She did. (*Singing the first line*) "Panis angelicus." Which I suppose would translate nowadays as angel delight. You really should come one Sunday, Albie. Just to hear her, I mean.

Albie You know me, Bernard. Neither religious, nor musical.

Bernard ⎫ (*speaking the all-too-familiar line together*) I don't really know
Albie ⎭ why Ruth married me.

Bernard starts to play a familiar tune, "The Foggy Foggy Dew"

Bernard (*singing quietly to his own accompaniment*)
> "When I was a bachelor I lived all alone,
> And I worked at the weaver's trade;
> And the only only thing
> That I ever did wrong
> Was to woo a fair young maid."

(*He continues playing the accompaniment as he speaks*) Roo isn't religious, you know. She just likes the tunes. It was the only constant element in our childhood, you see. Different homes, different pianos, but always the same songs.

Albie Did the British Council ever send you to Africa, Bernard?

Bernard I was posted to Addis for a while. Many many years ago.

Albie How was it?

Bernard Unbearable. The Ethiopians haven't got the idea at all. The whole point of going from a cool comfortable country like ours to a hot uncomfortable country like theirs is to feel one-up, surely. Their attitude to white men vacillates between indifference and contempt. Imagine my surprise. I advise you to stay at home.

Albie I'm not going to Ethiopia.

Bernard Where exactly are you going?

Albie Juba.

Bernard Juba? Remind me.

Albie looks round the room, and creates an imaginary map of Africa

Albie Right. I'm Cairo. The Mediterranean's out there. The Red Sea runs down the kitchen wall. You're Chad. The ottoman is Sudan. And Juba is the fire.

Bernard In Sudan?

Albie Yes. The extreme south. Zaire in the hall. Uganda in the front garden.

Ruth enters, and gets herself a drink

Bernard Well, well. What an adventure.

The phone rings

Bernard (*speaking to Ruth*) Albie's been mugging up on his African geography.

Sally comes running in, hoping the phone call is for her. She picks up the phone

Sally (*on the phone*) Yes? Oh, right.

Sally hands the phone to Albie, disappointed

It's Dr Hanlon.
Ruth It *is* Sunday, Albie.
Albie (*on the phone*) Mary ... Just having a drink before lunch ... Yes ...
Ruth (*explaining to Bernard*) Mary Hanlon runs this African doctor scheme.
Albie (*on the phone*) Yes. I talked to him yesterday ...
Bernard (*murmuring to Ruth*) Really, Roo, you should try harder.
Ruth What do you mean?
Albie (*on the phone*) No, the problem is the visa ...
Bernard Every time you talk about Albie's African trip you sound like poor old dada, "Can't complain, my dear."
Albie (*on the phone*) Hold on a moment, Mary.

Albie has trouble following his phone conversation while the others talk and laugh

Ruth (*in the manner of "poor old dada"*) "My joints have been acting up again—"
Bernard "But I can't complain, my dear."

Albie puts his hand over the receiver as he speaks to Ruth

Albie I'd better take this in the study.
Ruth Well, I can't complain, can I?

Albie gives Ruth the phone and exits

(*On the phone*) Dr Hanlon? I'm Ruth Steadman. Yes. I hope so ... (*She hears Albie pick up his extension*) Here he is. I'll leave him to you. (*She hangs up, and gives a shrug for Bernard*) I should be ashamed of myself. Of course he should go. Of course it's a good cause. It's not as if I can't manage without him.

There is the sound of a taxi off-stage

Ruth exits into the hall. There is the sound of the front door opening and closing

Sally That'll be Angus.
Bernard *The* Angus?
Sally Did you know Angus? Back then, I mean.

Bernard No, no. I wasn't even in the country. Where was I? Kingston, Jamaica, I think.

Sally But you know who he is?

Bernard I did receive a crumpled tear-stained letter.

They hear voices as Ruth and Angus enter the hall, off-stage

Sally (*hastening to give Bernard some vital information*) Angus doesn't talk, by the way.

Bernard Angus doesn't talk? Why ever not?

Sally Dad says it's an overdose of Zen. Apparently you have to listen for the sound of one hand clapping. After you've done that for a while, you forget how to talk.

Ruth enters, followed by Angus Ross. He is the same age as Albie, but a great deal bigger, and very good looking. His sheer size gives him an imposing physical presence, which is further enhanced by his disconcerting habit of staring at people without speaking

Ruth Albie's on the phone as usual.

Sally Hallo, Angus.

Angus embraces her

Angus Hi!

Ruth My brother, Bernard. He's staying with us.

Bernard Small derailment on the train of life. Roo has kindly offered me a siding. I find I have a natural talent for being a guest.

Ruth What do you want to drink, Angus?

Bernard The ideal guest should generate in his host a feeling of superiority without guilt. He should be just a little poorer——

Angus A beer, if you've got one.

Bernard Just a little less attractive——

Sally I'll get it.

Bernard And, if possible, unattached. Not unlike myself.

Sally exits to the kitchen

Ruth Bernard's like you, Angus. Never married, never wanted to be married. He resists being tidied up.

Sally enters with a can of beer for Angus

Bernard I don't resist at all. Somehow the broom has never passed my way.

Ruth Do shut up, Bernard.

Bernard Someone has to say something, Roo dear, it's traditional.

Sally You have to ask us how we are, Angus, or what's the news?, or something like that.

Angus What's the news?

Sally Dad's off to a refugee camp in Sudan.

Angus (*very surprised*) Sudan?

Ruth Just for three months. It's a sort of medical charity scheme.

Albie enters, his call over

Albie Angus!
Angus Albie!

They embrace

Albie Welcome. You haven't just come all the way from New Mexico, I hope?
Ruth He's in London for a few weeks.

A silence falls

Bernard finishes his drink and puts it down

Bernard (*addressing Angus*) Well now, I can see that you're bursting for a long cosy chat about old times.
Ruth Lunch in half an hour.
Bernard Shall I open the wine?
Ruth Yes, please.

Bernard exits

Albie (*taking in Angus properly*) Well. You look younger than ever, Angus. How on earth do you do it? Don't tell me. No stress. The happy hermit.
Ruth Angus isn't a hermit.
Albie He lives alone, doesn't he? In a house in the mountains, with a view across the valley of the Rio Grande all the way to——
Sally Summit Peak, where he sits on his porch every evening and watches the sun set over the valley.
Albie Is that still the scenario, Angus?
Angus Yes.
Albie How long does it take for the sun to set? Half an hour? More?
Angus More.
Albie Amazing.
Sally What's amazing about it?
Albie Being able to order your life so that you have time to watch the sun set every evening.
Ruth Albie's convinced that everyone else has more fun than him. I keep telling him the grass on the other side of the fence is astroturf.

Angus turns to look out of the window at the view

Albie You must say something about Ruth's view, Angus. She only bought the house for the view.
Sally He has seen it before, Dad.
Albie Surely it's not worn out already? We've still got twelve years to go on the mortgage.
Ruth (*speaking to Angus*) It's not the Rio Grande, but it's not bad, is it? I do love it, it's true. It's what I've dreamed of all my life, a house on a hill, with a high garden looking over a valley, and a river winding down to the sea.
Albie Houses are like dogs, you know. They only ever really have one owner. And it's certainly not me.

Ruth Oh, Albie, don't pretend you're not proud of it too.
Sally You'd better say something, Angus.

Albie and Sally watch Angus, to see if he will vouchsafe a rare word

Angus (*offering at last a tentative suggestion*) Wow?
Sally You don't sound very sure.
Angus Wow!
Ruth Thank you, Angus. Much appreciated. Now come and help me pick some asparagus for lunch. It's the first of the season.

> *Ruth and Angus exit*

Albie (*turning to Sally with a grin*) Do we count "wow" twice?
Sally Oh, yes.
Albie Then I make it five. "Albie. Yes. More. Wow? Wow!"
Sally Is that a record?
Albie Good God, no. For Angus that's almost chatty.

Sally sits down at her mother's desk and takes out her mother's make-up. She starts experimenting with Ruth's lipstick

Sally Dad? Do you think I should cut my hair?
Albie Cut your hair? How much?
Sally Really short. Like a lavatory brush.
Albie Why?
Sally I don't know. I can feel it coming over me.
Albie I'd just as soon you didn't.
Sally I knew you'd say that. What was Angus like when you first knew him?
Albie Pretty much the way he is now.
Sally What did Mum see in him?
Albie Ask her.
Sally The unattainable, I suppose.
Albie Thank you, Sally. Should you be doing that?
Sally Did he talk any more back then?
Albie Not much. And most of that was Zen aphorisms. "To the caterpillar, the butterfly is the end of the world." That sort of thing.
Sally What does that mean?
Albie You tell me.
Sally I told him you were going to Sudan. That made him speak.
Albie What did he say?
Sally "Sudan?!"
Albie That's what everyone says. Ten million people facing death by starvation, you say you might pop over and lend a hand, and they say, "Sudan?!"
Sally It does rather upstage the rest of us, actually, Dad: I mean, maybe we should all go to Africa, or live more simply and give our money to the poor. I would, too, except I don't want to.
Albie Everyone's different, darling. Everyone's even different from themselves too, if you know what I mean.
Sally Oh, yes, Dad. I'm completely different from myself. (*She looks at*

herself in the make-up mirror, and gets a momentary objective impression of her appearance) There, see! I'm not like that at all. It's all wrong. I'm going to start again.

Albie Why? You look great.

Sally You thought I looked great when I was ten.

Albie You did.

Sally I'm not ten any more, Dad.

Sally exits

Albie goes and stares thoughtfully at the fire. He puts another log on it

Angus enters and stands by the windows, with his back to the room. Albie does not see him and starts to speak aloud

Albie (*rehearsing his speech*) I thought, rather than make a speech, I'd tell you a story. It's a story about a boy who stayed at home. (*Turning*) I've taken to talking to myself these days. Cracking up fast, I suppose.

Angus says nothing

Albie does his best to make conversation unaided

I'm trying to remember when you were last here. Two years?

Angus nods

This not talking. Is it just a pose?

Angus If you like.

Albie I don't mind, speaking for myself, which is what you force me to do. But I should think it intimidates a lot of people. And even I can't help feeling, absurdly, for no good reason, that the less you say, the more it will be worth hearing, when and if you do speak.

Angus says nothing

We were at a dinner party the other day, Ruth and I, and there was a lull in the conversation, which terrified the hostess, so she came up with a party game question. "Do you ever wish you were someone else, and if so, who?" (*He pauses and looks at Angus enquiringly*)

After a moment's silence

Angus (*obligingly*) And do you?

Albie Yes, I wish I was someone else most of the time. For a start, who wants to be called Albert? What does it remind you of? The Albert Memorial, which is more or less what I am: a memorial to my maternal grandfather, Professor Albert Russell, whose name I bear. Albert Russell Steadman. A.R.S. (*He nods in sad acknowledgement*) At school it was Arse, Arsehole, Arselicker, Half-Arse. I've never forgiven my mother for that. Still, a minor matter, I suppose. Yes, I wish I was someone else. But ... (*He looks at Angus again*)

Angus says nothing

But who?, you ask. Ah, well, that's not so easy to answer. I want to be a man who is free to do just as he wants. Not unlike yourself, Angus. You're free to do just what you want, wouldn't you say?

Angus If you like.

Albie You don't have to think of other people. I do.

Angus seems by his expression to doubt this

No? Look at you and Ruth, twenty years ago or whenever it was. You go for a walk with her to wherever it was, and you tell her whatever it was you told her, and it broke her heart. You could have made her happy. Instead, you made her unhappy.

Angus does not dispute this

Don't get me wrong. I'm not saying you should have married her, just to make her happy. Maybe you shouldn't have let it get so far in the first place, that's another matter.

Albie looks at Angus, who says nothing. He takes out his wallet and produces a twenty-pound note

Let's put this on a commercial footing. I have a question. Am I entitled to seek my own happiness at the expense of other people's? Twenty pounds for a usable answer.

Angus smiles at this, and considers

Albie waits

Angus Other people's happiness isn't my responsibility.

Albie Other people's happiness isn't my responsibility? (*This strikes Albie forcibly. He says nothing for a few moments, and then holds out the note*)

Sally enters

Sally Dad, Mum says can you come and carve, please.

Angus takes the note, studies it, and pockets it

Sally, Angus and Albie exit

Lights fade on the Steadman home, and come up on Dr Mary Hanlon. She is giving a talk to a hall full of hospital doctors. She is an intense woman in her early thirties, neither plain nor pretty, but the conviction that illuminates her face as she speaks gives her presence real charisma

Mary This is not an appeal for money. It's an appeal for lives. I'm not here to ask you for charity, or to make you feel guilty. I'm here to ask you one simple question: are you leading the life you want to lead? If your answer is yes, then what I have to say won't be of any interest to you. You might as well leave now. I won't mind. (*She pauses, to see if anyone wants to leave*) No-one ever does leave. I used to think that meant everyone was eager to change their lives, but once, after I gave this talk in Hammersmith, a junior registrar came up to me and thanked me warmly, and when I said, "Will you be joining us in the camps?" He said no, he just felt so much better knowing there was somewhere worse than the Charing Cross Hospital. I work in a field hospital in a large refugee camp near a town called Juba, in the south of Sudan. The population of the camp divides crudely into three. One third is dying of starvation. Another third is seriously malnourished, and dying of infectious diseases; dysentery, cholera, typhoid. The final third is reasonably healthy, and killing each other in a civil war. So you won't be surprised to hear that the question I'm most often asked is, why bother? You read the papers. This year the drought is the worst ever, the disaster the largest ever. Ten million facing starvation; fifteen million. It's true, and at the same time, it's too much. The sheer scale of the tragedy makes people block their ears and shut their eyes. What can I say? That I'm bringing the suffering to an end? I wish I was. That I'm saving lives? A few, perhaps, but for what? For the war? For the famine? The truth is, I haven't got an answer. It's just become my work. It's what I do. But let me ask you the same question about your life. Why do you bother? Are you leading the life you want to lead? When it's over, will you look back and say, that wasn't what I meant to do at all? That's not how it is for me. For five years now I've known the greatest freedom life has to offer. If I die tomorrow, I'll be able to say, I lived the life I wanted to live. Will you?

As her speech ends, the Lights come up on an area that represents the office and warehouse of a charity organisation. There is a chair, a desk with piles of paper on it and stacks of boxes

Smithy, a warehouseman, enters pushing a trolley loaded with boxes

Mary Wotcha, Smithy.
Smithy Hallo, Doctor.

Andrew Rainer enters unannounced alongside the trolley. He is a middle-ranking official in the Foreign Office

Rainer Just a chat, really. Jeffreys—he looks after East Africa—Jeffreys thought the informal approach would go down best.
Mary A chat about what?
Rainer The political situation in the south of Sudan.
Mary I run a hospital. I'm not political.
Rainer Not political? That's a good one. Yes, I haven't heard that in quite a while.

Albie enters, dressed for his dinner. He sees Rainer, and not wanting to interrupt, backs off again

Albie I'm so sorry, Dr Hanlon——
Mary Russell. This is Mr——?
Rainer Rainer. Andrew Rainer.
Mary Dr Steadman.

Rainer offers Albie his hand

Rainer Dr Albert Steadman, yes?

Albie Yes.

Mary I think we'll find he's come to issue us with a government health warning.

Rainer She called you another name.

Albie Russell. My middle name. Some people use it.

Rainer You're going to Juba on a three month assignment?

Albie Is there a problem?

Rainer There's a civil war in the south. Juba is in the heart of the war zone. Is that a problem?

Mary He does know what's going on, Mr Rainer.

Rainer Really? Yes, I'm sure you do. Nor do we wish to discourage your admirable work in the region.

Mary But——?

Rainer Let's say, we can no longer guarantee your safety.

Mary If I wanted my safety guaranteed, I'd stay at home.

Rainer Very plucky. Yes. Chapeau. (*He raises an imaginary hat in homage and turns to Albie*) They call her "the angel of the camps", Jeffreys tells me. What will they call you? Angels are bi-sexual, I believe. No, that's not the word. Ambi-sexual? Neuter?

Albie I'm only going for three months, Mr Rainer. And I'm part of a team of—how many is it now? .

Mary Eighteen. Including auxiliaries.

Rainer And how many of those are British?

Mary Most of them. Ah, I see what this is about. (*She scribbles on a piece of paper as she explains to Albie*) A group of French aid workers were kidnapped last year.

Rainer We don't wish to appear ungrateful, but this government does not negotiate with hostage takers.

Mary I take full responsibility for myself, Mr Rainer. If I show any signs of turning into an embarrassment, you may quote me.

Mary gives Rainer the piece of paper

Rainer (*reading aloud*) "No deals. Leave me to rot. Mary Hanlon."

Mary Helpful?

Rainer puts the sheet of paper into one pocket with a sigh

Rainer I told Jeffreys it would be no use. These selfless types are very stubborn, I said. No, he said, she'll understand she has obligations to her country. Appeal to her patriotism. That made me laugh. Patriotism?, I said. She'll tell me she's a citizen of the world. Jeffreys said people don't talk like that any more, but Jeffreys leads a very sheltered life. In Wimbledon.

Mary Look on the bright side. They may botch the kidnapping and kill me by mistake.

Rainer There you are, you see. The media love that sort of thing. "Angel of the camps jokes in the face of death." You don't have any bonny little children, do you?

Mary No.

Rainer So it could be worse. Right, that's that, then, isn't it? And how about you, Dr Steadman? A daughter of sixteen, I believe?

Albie Dr Hanlon's very well known out there. I think we'll be all right.

Rainer "We'll be all right." The authentic voice of the British hero class. "Bit of a rumpus in the trenches, Colonel, but we'll be all right."

Albie It's got nothing to do with heroes. I've led a very sheltered life, and a rather insular one. This is my chance to give something back, that's all.

Rainer (*fixing Albie with his steady sceptical gaze*) Ye-es. You're a cardiologist, I believe.

Albie I'm a doctor. I'll make myself useful in whatever way I can. (*He looks at his watch, then at Mary*) Dr Hanlon. I only looked in to tell you the visa still isn't through.

Mary I'll chase it up. It'll be there, I guarantee it. You run.

Albie Right. Goodbye.

Rainer Good luck on your travels.

Albie exits

Rainer prepares to leave

Mary is back busying herself with her papers

Rainer Does that rather nice man know what he's doing? He's just not the type. You are, I can see that. You live on the edge. Very helpful for the rest of us, shows us where the edge is, so that we don't fall off. But not him, I think.

Mary You don't think you're presuming rather a lot on one short meeting, do you?

Rainer You don't think you're playing a rather dangerous game, do you?

Mary stops leafing through her papers, and meets Rainer's eye

Mary What game?

Rainer Transformation. "You too can have a meaningful life."

Mary Unlike yourself? And Jeffreys?

Rainer I didn't say that.

Mary Why not try it? Surprise yourself. Maybe you can be a hero too.

Rainer I'm afraid I don't have the legs for it.

Mary All right, maybe it is all just a game. Maybe Dr Steadman will go running home to mummy soon enough. But what if he doesn't? What if you're the one who's left behind in the nursery?

Rainer holds her amused eyes for a moment, then gives a lift of his shoulders

Rainer Maybe you're right. I was never a very brave boy. But then, it is a very big nursery. Goodbye.

Rainer exits

Mary looks after him for a moment, then gathers up some papers and exits herself

The Lights fade on the office and come up on the Steadman home. It is late at night

> *Ruth lies on the ottoman, writing in a red exercise book. A deed box is open on the floor, and in it there are many other similar red exercise books*

> *Albie enters, back from his dinner. He sits down beside Ruth*

Albie Writing your diary?
Ruth Yes. How was the farewell dinner?
Albie Lots of jokes on the theme of the heart doctor with the big heart. Surprising amount of resentment beneath the *bonhomie*.

He puts his arms round her

Ruth Sally's not home yet.
Albie She shouldn't be out this late.
Ruth Are you drunk, Albie? You are.

Albie reaches for one of Ruth's diary books

I'd rather you didn't read that.
Albie It's ancient history. Nineteen sixty-nine.
Ruth Even so. Albie. Please. (*She takes the diary back*)
Albie I've read it before, Ruth.

Ruth is surprised and a little shocked

Ruth When did you read it? You never asked me.
Albie Would you have let me?
Ruth No, I wouldn't. I practically don't read it myself. I feel all peculiar now. As if you'd burgled me.
Albie I read it ages ago. Years ago. It seemed important at the time. (*He gets the diary back, and carries it over to the lamp to read from it. He finds a typical passage*) "Angus didn't turn up, as usual. Why do I wait for him? Because I'm a blob. Why am I so blobbine? Because wanting Angus leads to blobbitude."
Ruth God, don't remind me.
Albie Pages and pages of pottiness about Angus.
Ruth I was eighteen, Albie. Be fair.

Albie looks at her, and remembers her back then. He comes over and kisses her

Albie You and Helen Lehmann coming down Fitzwilliam Street in the snow, like Russian princesses. You said, "So you're Albert", and every word made a puff of smoke. (*He returns to the lamp and reads from another part of the diary*) "Mass outing to *Fistful of Dollars* at the Rex. Angus loves Clint Eastwood because he never talks. He said if Clint would only stop shooting people he'd be a Zen master. Helen said, 'But are Zen masters good in bed?' I just smiled." Very Zen.
Ruth Please, Albie.
Albie Don't you find it interesting? I do.
Ruth It's not you who looks like a lemon.

Albie You don't think so? (*He reads from the diary again*) "A typical conversation with Albie. *Me:* 'So what do you want to do?' *Albie:* 'What do you feel like?' *Me:* 'Let's do what you want.' *Albie:* 'I want to do . . . something you'd like'."

Ruth That's enough, Albie. Put it back in the box. Please.

Albie Do you ever wonder if things could have turned out different? You could have stayed with Angus. He wouldn't have turned into a recluse.

Ruth It would never have worked.

Albie I would have married someone else, I suppose. And we'd all be different people.

Ruth Only you didn't, and we're not.

She puts the diaries back in the box and closes it. She sees Albie's melancholy mood, and goes and puts her arms round him

Stop it, please. Just stop this.

Albie I knew, by the way.

Ruth What?

Albie That you weren't in love with me back then.

Ruth (*upset by this information*) I'm sorry.

Albie I don't blame you. I wouldn't have fallen in love with me. Nobody falls in love with a poodle with low self-esteem.

Ruth You've changed. I've changed.

Albie Do you remember me saying to you once that I'd like to be called Russell? You said, "Don't be silly, Albie."

Ruth I've always known you as Albie. I married Albie, not Russell.

Albie I'd rather be Russell.

Ruth Why?

Albie I don't know. Albie's white, isn't it? Like albino. Russell's more reddish. Russet.

Ruth Rusty.

Albie I'd rather be Russell. (*He follows his late night line of thought, almost unaware that he is speaking aloud*) I was supposed to follow in my grandfather's footsteps. And bugger me, I have. But I don't want to be my grandfather. He was always old. I want to be young before I'm old.

Ruth is used to Albie's moods, and is only half attending, when he says something he has not said before

I want to leave, Ruth.

Ruth What?

Albie I'm restless.

Ruth Did you say you want to leave?

Albie Yes.

Ruth Leave what?

Albie Everything, really.

Ruth Everything?

Albie Yes.

Ruth This house?

Albie Yes.

Ruth Sally?

Albie She'll be leaving home soon. She's hardly here as it is.

Ruth I thought you loved this house.

Albie It's only a house.

Ruth I don't understand. Where's this come from? When did this happen?

Albie I just feel there's more.

Ruth More what?

Albie Of me. People do evolve. "To the caterpillar the butterfly is the end of the world" Angus. But it's not the end of the world. It's starting a new life.

Ruth Without Mrs Caterpillar.

Albie It could be the best thing for both of us.

Ruth (*stunned*) For both of us? Have we talked about this before? Tell me what I said, it seems to have slipped my mind.

Albie Ruth—I'm not what you want. I never have been. You know that. Good old Albie, he'll do, if all else fails.

Ruth Is there someone else?

Albie I shouldn't have said anything. It's very late. We're both very tired.

Ruth I might as well have the whole catastrophe at once.

Albie I think we should go to bed.

Ruth Please tell me if there's someone else. I have a right to know.

A car comes screeching up outside. They hear bright laughter, car doors slamming, and the yelled farewells of young people

Albie looks at his watch, and frowns with anger

Albie What the hell's Sally up to? She's only sixteen for God's sake.

Ruth Seventeen.

Albie It's not fair on us. Do you know these friends of hers?

Ruth It doesn't matter, Albie.

Sally enters, her shoes in her hands, and drunk. She is very surprised to see her parents

Sally What are you doing up?

Albie I was just going to ask you the same question.

Sally Oh, we've just been talking and stuff.

Albie So have we. Talking, and stuff.

Sally Is anything wrong?

Ruth No, darling. Nothing's wrong. Did you have a good time?

Sally Not bad. I'm totally smashed, actually. I was afraid I'd bang into things and wake you. (*She drops into a chair, and immediately begins to fall asleep*)

Albie Go to bed, Sally.

Sally Can't I sleep here?

Albie No, you can't. Do you know what time it is? Go to bed.

Sally (*rising reluctantly*) Night.

Albie Good-night.

Sally exits

There is a short silence

Ruth Well?

There is a pause

   Sally enters

Albie What?

Sally Shoes. (*She picks up her shoes and holds them out for him to see*) I wish I was small again, and you could carry me upstairs and tuck me into bed.

Ruth So do I, darling.

   Sally exits

   (*Staring at Albie*) So is there?

Albie You think I'm incapable of doing this on my own, don't you?

Ruth I just want to know.

Albie What for? What good would it do?

Ruth I don't want you to do good to me. I just want to know.

Albie finds it hard to know how to tell her

   So there is.

Albie In a way.

Ruth Who.

Albie I didn't mean to say any of this tonight.

Ruth So when did you mean to say it?

Albie When I got back.

Ruth You mean you've been planning this? Is it in your desk diary? "Go to Africa. Save lives. Fly home. Desert family."

Albie No. Of course not.

Ruth You're not still going to go to Africa?

Albie I have to. It's all arranged.

Ruth Who is it?

Albie It doesn't matter who she is.

Ruth It may not matter to you. It matters to me.

Albie I can't cancel the Africa trip. People are depending on me.

Ruth People? Aren't there people here? Don't we matter?

Albie Yes, of course.

Ruth But not as much?

Albie What good would it do if I didn't go to Africa now?

Ruth Well, there seems to be a bit of a problem at home. Maybe you could help, you do live here. You are mixed up in all this.

Albie I'm not sure that I can help.

Ruth Try.

Albie Do you want me to stay even if I don't want to stay?

She stares back at him in silence

Ruth (*after a pause*) Yes.

Albie You want me to stay out of duty?

Another terrible pause

Ruth Yes.

Albie looks at her in silence for a moment, and then turns away

Albie (*speaking in a voice that does not sound like him*) I'm not responsible for your happiness, Ruth.

Ruth stares at him as if he has become a stranger

The Lights go down on the Steadman home and come up on Mary Hanlon's London warehouse

> *Smithy enters pushing a trolley loaded with boxes*

> *Mary Hanlon follows, with a clipboard, checking off the contents of the boxes as Smithy calls them out*

Smithy Glideball Finewriter, write from the Heart. Faulty ink flow. One thousand.
Mary Chocolate Easter eggs, slightly cracked. One thousand.
Smithy Fun Socks, knee-length. Three hundred pairs, non-matching. Just what they need in Africa.
Mary They don't go to Africa, dopey. They get sold here, for cash.

Smithy takes out a union-jack sock

Smithy If they know your foot's nationality, they might take it hostage. You sure you want the rest?
Mary Everything makes us money, Smithy.
Smithy Ten thousand used Christmas cards? You're the boss.

> *Smithy exits*

> *Albie enters carrying a carton*

Mary takes it from him. He has been telling her about his conversation with Ruth in the night

Albie I'm sorry. I didn't mean it to happen. But it's happened.
Mary What's happened? Nothing's happened.
Albie Everything's happened. You know that as well as I do.
Mary All I know is, you're a good doctor, you're joining the team in Juba, you're a married man, and I didn't ask you to leave your wife.
Albie People get married without the first idea what they're doing. I was twenty-two when I married Ruth. I listened to Van Morrison, and drank Nescafé with sugar, and thought the Chinese had got it right. Now I listen to Mozart, and grind my own beans, and look what happened to communism! Why should I have got the right marriage? I got everything else wrong.

Mary can't help being touched

Mary I didn't know you liked Van Morrison.

Smithy enters with a carton of used Christmas cards

Smithy Used Christmas cards. Only one owner. (*He reads one of the cards with dry relish*) "Happy Christmas from Bob, Betty, the boys and Bongo. Woof woof."
Mary Thank you, Smithy.
Smithy There's more. Like, a lot more.
Mary We can recycle them.

Smithy exits

Albie All my life I've put other people first. All my life I've tried to be someone I'm not. Someone other people want me to be. I've never met anyone like you before. You don't ask anything of me. You give everything of yourself.
Mary No more, Russell. Please.
Albie I feel I'm who I really am with you. I know I haven't said this before. Not aloud.
Mary I'm not asking you to say any of it now.
Albie I've known it ever since I heard you make that speech of yours. Is it so wrong to want it?
Mary Yes. Yes.
Albie I don't give Ruth what she wants. Only a kind of security she thinks she needs. She needs to be released too. It could be the best thing for her in the end.
Mary Are you trying to tell me she doesn't love you?
Albie Ruth loves a lot of things. The family. The house. The garden. Singing. I'm on the list.

Mary makes a last attempt to head off what she so much longs for

Mary When we get to Juba, we're going to be working under very difficult conditions——
Albie I love you.
Mary —in very cramped conditions——
Albie I love you.
Mary —with a team around us——
Albie I love you.
Mary —and work to do—work——(*She falters into silence*)
Albie I love you.

Smithy enters, with another carton of used Christmas cards

Smithy All that used-up goodwill. Wears me out just thinking about it.
Mary Why not leave the rest till after lunch?

Smithy looks at his watch and brightens up with the thought of an early lunch

Smithy You're a true Christian, Doctor.

Smithy exits

Mary I think you'd better not come to Juba after all. It's not fair on the rest
of the team. Or me.
Albie If that's what you want.
Mary I got your visa through.
Albie There you are, then. I have to come with you now.

*With this, Mary's resistance suddenly gives way. Sweetly, helplessly, she gives
a small lift of her shoulders*

*Albie reaches out one hand and touches her cheek. She covers his hand with
hers, never taking her eyes from his*

Mary You know, don't you? I've not done this before. Given all of myself
to one person. I'll go all the way with you.
Albie I'll go all the way with you too.
Mary That was school. "How far did you go? Did you go all the way?"
Albie How far did you go?
Mary I went to Africa. I went precisely nowhere. I was far too scared. And
proud, I suppose. I knew it wasn't meant to be like that.

*He takes her in his arms. She resists no more. She kisses him fully and
intensely*

It was meant to be like this.

Albie and Mary kiss again

> *The Lights come up on Ruth Steadman, standing alone, poised to sing. The
> organ plays the introduction to Vivaldi's "Domine Deus", and she begins to
> sing. She sings with intense feeling*

*As she does so, Albie and Mary's embrace becomes more and more passionate.
Without either of them removing any clothes, their contact becomes sexual.
Mary especially yields up her entire body to the embrace*

*The lyrical intensity of Ruth's singing both matches and counterpoints this
silent passion*

> *Slowly the Lights on the embracing couple and Ruth fade to Black-out*

When the anthem finishes, the Lights come up on a cliff top

> *Angus enters with Ruth. She has been confiding in him as they walk along
> the cliffs*

Ruth You think it's childish, don't you? Needing someone else so much.
Angus Not childish. Dangerous.
Ruth Dangerous? I like that. Marriage as a jungle, through which we go
naked. Adam and Eve and poisonous snakes. I am quite frightened,
actually, Angus.

He puts one arm around her, as if to protect her

Thank you.

She turns and looks into his eyes as he holds her. He smiles

Why don't you talk any more? You used to talk.

Angus What do you want me to say?

Ruth You say, he can't do this to you.

Angus "He can't do this to you."

Ruth There isn't anything to say. That's what's so bloody about it. There's another woman, of course. He won't tell me who, but I can guess. It'll be some little nurse whose only object in life is to devote herself to his happiness.

Angus looks at her, and she finds some kind of sympathy in his eyes

You'll keep my secret, won't you, Angus?

Angus Of course.

Ruth Things are bad. Albie said to me, "Do you want me to stay even if I don't want to?" That's a terrible question. Whatever way I answer, I lose. I want to say, happiness isn't enough.

Angus Even, love isn't enough?

Ruth But then, what is? Maybe it doesn't exist. Maybe everyone should do whatever they want. Like Albie.

Angus Like me?

She looks at him, trying to make out his reaction to her

Ruth Did you ever love me?

Angus Yes.

Ruth But loving me didn't mean wanting to stay with me. I'm not complaining. I'm trying to understand. For me, loving someone means wanting to build a world with them. Is that just me? Does everyone else carry love around with them like an overnight bag? Doesn't marriage matter any more?

Angus is not sure how to respond

Ruth prompts him with a tiny nod of her head

Angus Yes. It does.

Ruth He loves her, whoever it is, and he thinks that's all that matters. I'm supposed to say, oh well, if you love her, then of course our marriage is an empty shell, and love is the pearl, isn't it?

Angus looks for his cue

Ruth shakes her head

Angus No. It isn't.

Ruth What can I say for poor dowdy marriage against the glamour of love? Marriage is just an arrangement, isn't it? It's just about property and home decorating and staving off loneliness, isn't it?

Angus is on to this one

Angus No. It isn't.

Ruth I wish you didn't have to go back to Santa Fe, Angus. Who else can I talk to like this?

Angus Brother Bernard?

Ruth Bernard? I wish I could. Bernard had a breakdown, you know. More like a head-on collision, really. He was a total write-off for a while. Now he's what he calls "wobbly". He can't take other people's troubles, they make him wobble.

Angus What will you do if Albie does leave?

Ruth Form a biker gang called the Wives of Hell. Roar about the countryside dressed in black leather beating up men like Albie with bicycle chains.

Angus grins

(*Sighing*) If only. Do you think I'm one of those women who men leave?

Angus No.

Ruth Two out of two.

Angus Over twenty years ago, Ruth.

Ruth It's still a hundred per cent failure rate. You did it on a walk, pretty much like this. Remember? (*She rises and starts to gather up the picnic things*) An al fresco dumping.

Angus I don't have to go back to Santa Fe. I don't have to do anything.

Ruth Then don't. (*She walks away*)

Angus Hang on, Ruth. I've got something else to say.

Ruth exits

Angus exits after her

The Lights come up on the Steadman home. It is early morning

Albie sits on the piano stool, with his luggage before him

Ruth enters with a tray of tea

Albie The taxi'll be here soon.

Ruth Right. Did you check the flight? Is it on time?

Albie Yes. As far as Cairo, at least.

Ruth Remember that night we spent at Gatwick? Where were we going?

Albie Venice.

Ruth That's right, Venice. Eleven hours in Gatwick departure lounge, then that hotel.

Albie The hotel was a mistake.

Ruth It wasn't a bad holiday.

Albie Just too expensive.

Ruth You kept getting your calculator out and converting the prices into pounds and saying, Jesus Christ, two pounds for a capuccino! (*She begins to cry*)

Albie It's only for three months, Ruth.

Ruth How do I reach you?

Albie I've left the address on your desk, and the number of the London office. There's another number there, for the oil. They should be coming to top up the tank in a month or so, but it's just in case.

Ruth How long will the oil last?

Albie Six weeks. (*He checks his watch*) The taxi's late. I said six-thirty sharp.

Ruth You've got plenty of time.

Albie I have to be on this flight. The connection at Cairo's very tight.

Ruth You've never missed a plane in your life.

Albie What if they've forgotten? It'll take at least half an hour to get another taxi out here.

Ruth Please don't go. Please.

Albie There probably wouldn't even be a taxi available this early. (*He goes to the phone*) I can't change my plans at the last minute, Ruth. What the hell's the number of that taxi firm? Eight-nine-nine . . . ?

Ruth Have you told Sally?

Albie Eight-nine-nine, two-three something. Have I told Sally what?

Ruth Do you want me to? Eight-nine-nine, three-two-five.

He dials the number

Albie No, I don't want you to tell Sally.

Ruth I want Sally to know, Albie. It's not fair on me. How am I supposed to keep it a secret from her that you've left us?

Albie I'm in Africa. What's so difficult about that? (*On the phone*) Hello? Dr Steadman here. I ordered a cab for six-thirty . . . Right . . . Well, it isn't . . . Yes, all right. Thank you . . . Yes, of course. Bye. (*He hangs up, frowning*) It should be here by now. Probably crashed on the way.

Ruth So will you tell her?

Albie The taxi's going to be here any second, she's asleep upstairs, and you want me to wake her up and tell her—tell her——

A taxi pulls up outside and gives two low parps on its horn

There is a short silence

Five minutes late.

Ruth Don't go, Albie.

Albie Of course I'm going. Look: luggage, ticket.

Ruth If you go now, you'll kill me.

Albie Don't be ridiculous. Nobody's killing anybody. I'm getting a taxi, that's all.

Ruth You think you can run away from everything you don't like, but you can't.

Albie I don't want you to tell Sally anything. I'll talk to her when I get back.

Ruth Please. Look at me. Please.

Albie I'm going now. (*He starts to leave*)

Ruth I'd rather you died than left me like this.

Albie comes to a stop

If you were dead, at least I could mourn you. You'd be gone, but I could remember the years we had together. If you leave me for another women, you take those years too. I would rather you were dead.

The taxi hoots again, more impatiently

Bernard enters

Bernard I think there's a taxi waiting.
Ruth Run away, then.
Albie It's costing enough as it is.
Ruth You don't have to take it.
Albie I still have to pay.
Ruth Who are you?
Albie I have to go, Ruth.
Ruth No, you don't. It's only what you want. You're only doing what you want.
Albie How else am I to know what to do?

Ruth stares at Albie, appalled

The taxi hoots again

Albie half runs towards the door, uncertain how to leave

Albie So. Goodbye?
Ruth Ring me to let me know you've arrived safely.
Albie Right.

She turns away and bows her head

Ruth You'd better go, if you're going.

Albie still lingers

The taxi hoots one last time

Bernard Bon voyage?
Albie Thank you, Bernard.

Albie shakes Bernard's offered hand. He gives Ruth a last look, but she does not look up

Goodbye, then.

Sally enters, very sleepy

Albie takes her in his arms

Sally Why do you have to go in the middle of the night, Dad?
Albie It's not the middle of the night. It's morning. Look, daylight.
Sally Oh, yes.
Albie I'll miss you, sweetheart.
Sally You'll be back for my birthday, won't you?

Albie frowns, briefly thrown by this

You can't remember when it is!

Albie Of course I can. June twenty-sixth. Come on.

Albie exits with Sally

Bernard I'm glad I was in time to wave our traveller on his way.

Sally enters and makes her way back to bed

Sally Up the wooden hill to Bedfordshire.

Sally exits

Bernard Travel is a vice, you know. I used to give way to it all the time. Now that I'm older and wiser I see that it's all a terrible mistake, this coming and going. People should either stay where they are, or go away and not come back.

Ruth doesn't speak

Bit down, are you, Roo?
Ruth Just a bit.
Bernard Would you like the going away song, or the coming home song?
Ruth Coming home. (*She sits on the sofa*)

Bernard starts to play a soft tune, as if for his own pleasure

Bernard (*singing in his sweet light voice*)
                    "So we'll go no more a-roving
                    So late into the night——"
(*He breaks off to speak to her quietly*) Just you and me, Roo. Like it used to be. (*He continues to sing*)
                    "Though the heart be still as loving
                    And the moon be still as bright."
Ruth He thinks I didn't love him. When we were first married.
Bernard Is he right?
Ruth Maybe.
Bernard (*singing*)   "For the sword outwears its sheath,
                    And the soul wears out the breast,
                    And the heart must pause to breathe,
                    And love itself have rest . . ."
Ruth I do love him, Bernard. More than he thought, certainly. More than I thought, but I seem to have got the timing wrong.
Bernard One only really wants things when they're taken away.
Ruth Do you think that's all it is?
Bernard I can't say, Roo. Albie is an acquired taste.
Ruth He was sweet with Sally, when she was little. She had trouble going to sleep, just childish fears, she said the walls made faces in the dark. So Albie sat on the stairs outside her room, and every now and again she'd call out, "Daddy, are you there?", and he'd say, "Here I am." (*This memory makes her smile even as it hurts her*)
Bernard (*completing the song*)
                    "Though the night was made for loving,

And the day returns too soon,
Yet we'll go no more a-roving
By the light of the moon." (*He plays himself out*)

Ruth I think something happens to people when they live together for a long time. Almost without them knowing. I want to call it love, but it's not what everyone else calls love. It's more like the feeling you have about your home. You don't realize it till you go away, and then you get homesick.

Bernard These little sicknesses do pass. (*He starts to make himself a drink*)

Suddenly the pain and powerlessness of her situation sweeps over her, and she begins to weep

Ruth Does it matter if the reasons were wrong in the beginning? It shouldn't matter. It's what happens afterwards, all those days and hours and years together afterwards. Don't they count? (*She looks at Bernard*)

Bernard has his back to her as he makes his drink

You don't want to hear this, do you?

Bernard Bit wobbly. Can't quite manage the details.

Ruth There's so much I want to say to him.

Bernard You can always write him a letter.

Ruth "Dear Albie. I can't sleep. The walls are making faces. Are you there?"

Bernard goes to her, and sits beside her

Bernard Here I am.

The Lights cross-fade and come up on another part of the stage: a room in a staff bungalow in Africa

There is a wide bed, covered in a mosquito net, through which little can be seen clearly, except that two people (Albie and Mary) are lying there together

It is night-time

A figure appears in the African room, more a shadow than a person. Suddenly he strikes, seizing one of the people in the netted bed. It is Albie

As Albie struggles in his captor's grip, the other person in the bed becomes visible. It is Mary Hanlon

We hear no sound, nor do we see any of them distinctly: the moment has the quality of a dream, or rather, a nightmare, because both are powerless to prevent what is happening, as Albie is drawn inexorably out of sight

Fade to Black-out

ACT II

The Lights come up on a television studio

Mary Hanlon is being made up by a make-up girl, before appearing on a television chat show

Andrew Rainer enters

Rainer Dr Hanlon? Another fifteen minutes of fame?

Mary Am I sharing the limelight with you, Mr Rainer?

Rainer Oh, no, I'm here in a purely advisory capacity. And the pleasure of a few words with you.

Mary Is there any news? No.

Rainer I'm afraid not. I've tried to explain that this kind of publicity doesn't help the process of negotiation, but apparently once events become news, the people cannot be denied.

Mary What process of negotiation?

Rainer There are little arrangements that can be made without loss of face on either side, as long as they remain private. Not very private, television, is it? But then, you are so good at it.

Mary Are you negotiating?

Rainer The situation is delicate——

Mary (*quietly angry*) Colonel Kurun is a gangster. He's a dealer. He'd do a deal tomorrow if you offered him something.

Rainer He's a gangster who calls his gang the People's Freedom Militia, which complicates matters.

Mary Make him a gesture. Let him get something out of it. That's all he wants.

Rainer A supportive gesture to a group who are in rebellion against the government of the country?

Mary A government that's starving its own people into submission?

Rainer They are now allowing food aid into the south. We can't afford to antagonise the Khartoum government at this moment.

Mary So try cash.

Rainer Cash? How much do you suggest we offer?

Mary A thousand dollars? He'd take it.

Rainer So we buy one man for a thousand dollars. Next time they take two, and get two thousand dollars.

Mary And terrorism must never be seen to pay.

Rainer Terrorism doesn't pay.

Mary Of course terrorism pays. Half the world's leaders were terrorists once. In twenty years' time, Colonel Kurun could be an honoured statesman, the man who led his people to freedom. And if he is, won't you

be there with the red carpet and the trade delegation and the greetings
from the Queen?

Rainer takes a piece of paper from one pocket

Rainer (*reading*) "No deals. Leave me to rot. Mary Hanlon." Is it your view
that Dr Steadman is less capable of sacrifice than you are yourself?

Mary Oh, really, Mr Rainer.

Rainer You're not his mother, Dr Hanlon. He's not a child. I'm aware that
you'd like to do his suffering for him, but I'm afraid that can't be
arranged.

Ruth enters, led by a studio AFM

Rainer (*introducing himself to Ruth*) Mrs Steadman. Andrew Rainer. We
have spoken on the phone.

Ruth Yes.

Rainer Do you know Dr Hanlon?

Ruth looks at Mary in surprise. She is not as she had expected

Ruth Dr Hanlon? No.

Mary We haven't actually met before. I was told you'd said no to this.

Ruth I did. She's very persistent. (*To Rainer*) Is there any news?

Rainer Not as yet. Everything that can be done is being done. You'll be the
first to know. They'll be waiting for me upstairs. I shall leave you in the
tender hands of the great British public.

Rainer exits

Mary He wants me to shut up, but the simple fact is, I'm responsible for
what happened.

Ruth Albie did what he did for his own reasons.

Mary It should have been me. They probably would have taken me too,
except I'm a woman. Women don't have much value out there.

Ruth No. I suppose not.

June Armitage enters. She wears an ear-piece

June Dr Hanlon. Nice to see you again. Mrs Steadman. June Armitage.
Forgive me for not being here to greet you. I was taping a short
introduction to our segment. I like to keep the introduction short, but at
the same time I try to capture the key idea. I asked myself one question.
Why has this story touched so many people? What is it about this man
that has produced such an outpouring of concern, and admiration, and
love? Mrs Steadman—may I call you Ruth?

Ruth Yes.

June I know how much you dislike all this media circus. I just want to say
two things to you. It won't take long. And it really could help.

Ruth What is it you want me to do?

June Just talk, that's all. No plan, no list of questions, that's not how I do
things. If you want to steer me in another direction, you can. You're in
charge. If we lose our way, we can always edit it later, you see? (*She loses*

sound in her ear-piece, and is briefly thrown) Robin? Where are you, Robin? I've lost you. I'm so sorry, we seem to have a gremlin in the talkback. I'll love you and leave you for thirty seconds.

June exits

Mary I'm glad you changed your mind. We need all the publicity we can get.
Ruth (*watching Mary throughout the following exchange*) You seem to have been rather better at that than me.
Mary People forget so quickly.
Ruth Please don't think I'm not grateful. I am.
Mary You do know that it could all go on for a long time.
Ruth So they told me.
Mary Did they say, "Some come back, some don't, some haven't been heard of for years"?
Ruth And nobody knows if they're alive or dead.
Mary Oh, no. I don't think Russell's dead.
Ruth (*saying without anger, what has become so obvious to her*) It is you, isn't it?

Before Mary can respond:

The studio AFM and June enter

June Right. We're all set now. (*She takes her seat, cushioning them in a stream of talk, with only occasional asides to the unseen producer*) It's all very informal, we don't go in for count-downs and so on, it only makes everyone tense. They'll tell me in my ear-piece when they're ready, and we just talk. Yes, Robin. Of course I will. Don't I always? Before we start, I have to make sure everyone can hear you. That doesn't mean you have to speak louder, just that they move the microphones closer. Ruth; what do you think of our chairs? We've had raging arguments over them.

June ushers Ruth and Mary to sit

Ruth Your chairs?
June They're supposed to create a relaxed, at-home sort of feeling. At whose home?, I'd like to know.
Ruth I don't know. They seem fine.
June I see I can't lure you into indiscretion on the furnishings. Dr Hanlon?
Mary (*baffled*) You want to know what I think of the chairs?
June (*listening to her ear-piece*) Yes. Right. Of course. Thank you, Robin. Switch yourself off, now, please. Right, all's well in the engine room, they tell me. Wouldn't it be lovely if one could switch everybody off like that? So, where are we? We are at speed. Five, four, three, two, one.

The programme's opening music plays and then fades

June (*speaking to the camera*) Albert Steadman is a new kind of hostage, the victim of a brand of kidnapping that has a peculiar power to shock, because it violates a fundamental law: he is the Good Samaritan mugged

by the man he has stopped to help. (*Turning to Ruth*) Mrs Steadman.
Ruth. Why was it that your husband went to Africa in the first place?

Ruth looks at Mary, but can't speak

As a doctor, he was involved in medical work, of course. On a voluntary
basis, I think?
Ruth Yes.

June Armitage sees that Ruth is too nervous for the moment

June (*turning to Mary*) In response to your appeal, Dr Hanlon?
Mary Yes. For some years now, I've been running a small field hospital in
one of the refugee camps.
June (*trying Ruth again*) What sort of man is your husband, Ruth?

There is a pause

Ruth I don't know.
June I know what you mean. The closer they are, the less we know how to
describe them. Perhaps I should ask Dr Hanlon that question. You
worked alongside him.
Mary For a short time.
June I get the impression of a modest man.
Mary Yes.
June Brave?

*Mary finds this very hard; but most of all she wants to speak the truth about
the man she loves*

Mary I don't think he would have thought himself brave. But he could have
stayed at home, and he chose not to. I'd say that takes courage.
June But not the obvious hero type?
Mary No.
June You were there when he was kidnapped?
Mary Yes.
June Did you see it happen?
Mary No. I was taking a shower.
June What exactly did happen?
Mary It was night. He was in bed——
June Is this in a tent?
Mary No. There are staff bungalows. They came into the bungalow. I
suppose the door had been left open. I think they were looking for
something to steal. And they stumbled on to Russell.
June So you don't think they came with the intention of kidnapping him?
Mary I don't think so.
June Do you think they even knew who he was?
Mary I'm sure they didn't.
June I noticed you call him Russell.
Mary He said he'd never liked the name Albie.

Ruth stares at her

June Perhaps I can come back to you, Ruth. How did you get the news of your husband's kidnapping?
Ruth A phone call.
June What was your first reaction to that call?

There is a pause

Ruth (*still staring at Mary*) I can't describe my reaction.
June What were your dominant feelings?
Ruth Anger. Fear.
June What was it you were afraid of?
Ruth (*still looking at Mary as she answers*) Of growing old alone.
June Do you feel alone now?
Ruth Yes.
June You're not alone, you know. Every woman in the country is feeling a little of what you're feeling now.
Ruth Do you think so? (*She still stares at Mary*)

Mary speaks to her directly, unable to take the situation any more

Mary Shall we stop this?
June Ruth? Do you want to stop?

Ruth nods

June Armitage makes a sign to her producer

   No sooner said than done. We all understand
Ruth Do you?
June Thank you, Robin. Right, we're not recording any more. It's all over. Does anyone feel the need of a stiff drink?
Ruth Yes.
June That we can manage.

June leads Ruth to a drinks trolley

   I know just what you're feeling. "Why must I expose myself to strangers? How fast can I get out of this place? Make them stop asking me questions." I suggest you help yourself. I think we have just about everything. Robin, ask Tom to order two cabs right away, will you? Thank you.

Ruth makes herself a strong drink

June Armitage moves to one side with Mary Hanlon

   (*Speaking to Mary quietly*) Thank you for that, Dr Hanlon. You were quite right. And don't worry that we may not have enough for the programme. Silence is golden, as they say. Those heart-breaking pauses. (*She goes back to Ruth*) Mrs Steadman—Ruth—I'm going to love you and leave you. We've ordered you a taxi, it won't be long, so now you can just switch me off. No need to say anything. I don't know much, but I know when I'm no longer required. (*She gives a nod to Mary*)

June exits

Ruth drinks her drink

They do not speak for a few moments

Mary If you hate me, say you hate me.

Ruth You were taking a shower? (*For a moment it seems she'll say no more; but she can't hold it back*) I hate you. I wish Albie had never met you. I wish you'd never been born.

Mary is shocked by the quiet bitterness in Ruth's voice

Mary Will you let me try to explain?

Ruth Don't bother. I know. You never meant it to happen. It was cruel fate.

Mary This isn't meant as an excuse, but there's a part of me that doesn't work very well, and never has. I don't have that trick of intimacy.

Ruth What on earth is that?

Mary I'm no good with men. Every date I've ever had with a single man has been a nightmare. I know I'll screw it up and blame myself afterwards, because that's what happens every time. So I freeze and I sweat and I screw it up, and I blame myself afterwards.

Ruth is bewildered by this adolescent confession, as heartfelt as it is inappropriate

Ruth How old are you?

Mary I know, there's nothing you can tell me about this. I'm thirty-five, and I can't act normally with men. Unless they're gay, or unless they're married.

Ruth So marriage was your chaperone. Great. (*Ruth looks at Mary properly, studying her appearance*) Did Albie tell you you have beautiful eyes?

Mary says nothing, but Ruth sees she has guessed right

And great legs?

Mary turns away

He never was very original with his compliments.

Mary I do believe he loves me.

Ruth Yes, you're the woman he loves. I'm the one he's left behind. You can sit by your lamp in the window and wait for him to come home. I can't. He isn't coming home to me. I'd rather he was dead.

Mary You don't mean that.

Ruth Albie used to tell me I had beautiful eyes, and great legs. He knew he was on safe ground there, eyes and legs. Even so, I liked it when he said it. Now you have them, the beautiful eyes, the great legs. You blind me, Dr Hanlon, and you cripple me. I don't even know that I want him to be released.

Mary Do you think I didn't care that he was married? I hated it. But it happened, and I couldn't stop it.

Ruth What happened? Love? The whirlwind?

Mary You don't know anything about me, but you still judge me.

Ruth Jesus, you want it all, don't you? You want Albie, and true love, and you still want to think well of yourself.

Mary I don't want to think well of myself. (*She now wants more than anything to explain herself to Ruth*) I'm glad you know. No more pretending. I'm no good at it anyway.

Ruth You seem to have managed.

Mary All right, I'll tell you.

Ruth Don't bother please.

Mary He told me you didn't love him.

Ruth He was wrong.

Mary He told me the marriage was over.

Ruth Not for me.

Mary I didn't know that.

Ruth Marriage means nothing, does it? Only love. Nothing else matters.

June enters

Ruth sees June Armitage entering, and turns and exits

June We've just been told that the traffic's locked solid all the way back to Marble Arch—oh . . .

Mary Do you mind if I don't take that taxi? I'd prefer the tube.

Mary exits

June Thank you, studio. Robin? I'm coming up.

June exits

The Lights cross-fade and come up on the Steadman home

Bernard is sitting at the piano, playing to himself

Ruth enters and takes off her coat

Bernard gives her a little nod of greeting and starts to play Novello's "Till the Boys Come Home". After the first verse Ruth is unable to control her feelings any more. She starts to weep

Ruth They want me to cry on television. They don't say so, but it's what they want. That's hard. I feel as if I have to pay the ransom. I have to buy Albie back with public grief.

Bernard I wish they'd ask me. The long, lonely agony of the brother-in-law? No, I suppose not. (*He starts to play again, speaking between the lines*) . . . I'd like to be able to say something helpful, but my mind seems to be cluttered with commonplaces . . . While there's life there's hope . . . But while there's life there's despair . . .

Ruth I can't do it any more, Bernard. The bravely smiling wife, I mean. I can't.

Bernard No need. They know the script already, it's always the same. Passion, crucifixion, resurrection. Suffering, acceptance, new life.

Ruth Tell me about the new life.

Bernard Oh, anything will do, just so long as it demonstrates that everything turns out for the best. You find you've lost weight. You fit all your frocks again. You write a book about life-changing crises. *Tragedy: the Diet.*

Ruth Oh, Bernard.

Bernard I'd be more sympathetic if only I had the knack.

Ruth It would almost be easier if I knew he was never coming back. Do you think he's gone for ever?

Bernard What do I know? People are impermanent, in my experience. Spare me the details, but what's he done?

Ruth What do you think? People do it all the time, I'm told. Just the usual everyday heartbreak. Albie left me.

Bernard For—someone else?

Ruth For someone else.

Bernard (*mystified*) An African?

Ruth (*laughing*) No. Before. (*Putting her arms round him*) Do you know, there hasn't been a single moment of my life when I didn't know you were there?

Bernard Do you remember how I used to be bigger and stronger than you were? Then we all grew up, and my hair fell out and my life fell apart, and you were bigger and stronger than me. Now we're getting back to the old arrangements. I like that much better.

Ruth I was so pleased that you came here, when things were bad for you.

Bernard I know I should have gone long ago. Every morning I say to myself. Come on now, pull yourself together, you're not a child any more, time to go back out into the big wide world. And every night I say, not yet, one more night of safety.

Ruth You call this safety? This is an earthquake zone. (*She turns and sees the view*) Hallo, view. Still there.

Bernard Why wouldn't it be?

Ruth I don't know. I've rather lost interest in it recently. I used to love it so much.

Ruth and Bernard exit

The Lights fade and come up on Albie in Africa

He is in a cage and in chains. He has had no access to washing or shaving facilities for some time, and it shows. He sits cross-legged on the earth, drawing a map in the dust with one finger, and murmuring to himself

Albie The A twenty-seven, Lewes. The A two-five-nine, Eastbourne. The Golden Galleon. Seaford. The river runs past Hailsham and Michelham, past Arlington to Alfriston, and down to the sea. The Seven Sisters. Right, the Seven Sisters. Haven Brow, Rough Brow, Short Brow. Brass Point. Flat Hill. One, two, three, four, five.

A sound beyond the cage, perhaps a man settling down onto a chair

Albie hears instantly

Albie (*alert*) Danny? Are you there? Danny? I've thought of another joke. Do you want to hear it? (*There is no answer, but Albie suspects Danny is* *listening*) There's a scorpion wants to cross a river, so he asks this frog to carry him across. "You must be joking", says the frog, "If you get on my back, you'll sting me, and I'll drown." "I won't do that", says the scorpion, "If I sting you, we'll both drown." The frog thinks about it. "All right", he says, so the scorpion gets on the frog's back, and they both go swimming across the river. Half-way across, the scorpion stings the frog, and they both start to drown. "What did you do that for?", says the frog, "You said you wouldn't sting me." The scorpion says, "I guess that's just how I am."

There is silence

Get it?

The Lights fade on Albie, and he is gone

The organ plays the introduction to "In Paradisum", from Fauré's Requiem

The Lights come up on Ruth Steadman as she begins to sing

Ruth   "In paradisum
                                       Deducant angeli . . ." (*She falters and comes to a stop*)

The organ and choir continue

Ruth struggles to regain control of herself, and begins to sing again, picking up at a later point

                                       "Te perducant te
                                       In civitatem sanctam
                                       Jerusalem . . ."

She stops again, stifling a scream. She turns her head away, struggles once more, and then gives up

Ruth exits

The Lights cross-fade and come up on the Steadman home

Sally enters, with Angus

Sally has had her hair cut very short

Sally I've been wanting to do it for ages. I'm a different person, aren't I? I catch sight of myself in a mirror and I don't know who it is. Think of that! I can be whoever I want. (*She poses for Angus*) I only had it done last night. Mum's not seen it. I've been trying on new clothes. I'm going to be so different. Maybe I'll change my name. Angus? You do like it?
Angus Yes. I do.
Sally Feel it.

Angus strokes her hair

Doesn't that give you a buzz? (*She strokes her own hair*) Bzz-bzz-bzz. Mum'll be back from church soon. There's no news, if you were going to ask. We don't talk about it much any more, actually. You run out of things to say.

Bernard enters. He is back from church

Bernard Is Roo back?
Sally No. Hasn't she been in church with you?
Bernard She started, but she didn't finish.
Sally What do you mean?
Bernard I'm sure she's fine.
Sally Fine? How come everybody's so fine?
Bernard Do I smell nothing roasting? It is Sunday, and very nearly lunchtime.
Sally You know Mum's line these days, "If you want food, there's the kitchen." Pity there isn't any food.
Bernard There's something different about you, isn't there?
Sally Ha ha, baldy.

Sally goes out to the kitchen

Bernard offers Angus his hand by way of greeting, not expecting him to say anything.

(*off*) I hate it when people say they're fine, especially Mum. If you feel lousy, why not say so?

Sally enters with a large bag of crisps

Look what I found. Why doesn't she talk about it?
Bernard I do wonder where she is.
Sally Probably getting consoled by the vicar. It's all part of God's plan, so no need to worry.
Bernard You've clearly never spoken to your vicar.
Sally Should I?
Bernard He suffers from depression.
Sally Jesus Christ.
Bernard Him too.
Sally What?
Bernard Jesus was a depressive. Two major breakdowns, one in the desert, one in the garden of Gethsemane. That's what's so clever about Christianity, there's one overall design, but you can assemble the units to suit your own particular needs; like a fitted kitchen.

There is the sound of the front door opening and closing

Sally That's Mum. Don't tell her I'm in. I want to surprise her. (*She hides under the piano*)

Ruth enters

Bernard She that was lost is found.
Ruth Don't count on it.
Bernard Where have you been?
Ruth Walking. Angus. How are you?
Angus Fine.

Bernard Did some wild-eyed optimist give you the impression there might be lunch?

Angus More or less.

Bernard I'd better go and do something about it.

Bernard exits to the kitchen

Ruth Anything new with you?

Angus No. Nothing new.

Ruth Nor me. No Albie, as you see. Not that there would be, even if there was. I know who she is, by the way. Whoever-it-is. Albie's other woman.

Sally comes out from under the piano

Ruth becomes aware of Sally from Angus's face. She turns and gets a double shock: that Sally has overheard her, and that she has cut her hair

Sally! Good God! What have you done?

Sally What's Dad done?

Ruth Darling, what possessed you to cut off all your lovely hair?

Sally Was Dad having an affair?

Ruth Yes.

Sally When?

Ruth Before he went away.

Sally Was it serious?

Ruth Yes.

Sally Why didn't you tell me?

Ruth looks at her daughter helplessly

Ruth I don't know. It all happened so quickly. Then—then he was gone. There didn't seem any point.

Sally Who was it?

Ruth Mary Hanlon.

Sally Dr Mary Hanlon! So he wasn't ever coming home anyway.

Ruth I don't know what he was going to do.

Sally Well, he wasn't bringing Mary Hanlon to live here, was he?

Ruth Darling ... (*But she cannot think what to say*) I wish you hadn't cut your lovely hair.

Sally Home should go on being the same. I'm sorry. I suppose that's childish. (*She kisses Ruth on one cheek, in a clumsy gesture of sympathy*) Don't worry about the haircut. It'll grow.

Sally exits into the kitchen

Ruth She's right, I should have told her. But what do I tell her? Things change. Men leave. Do I tell her everything you've ever loved you've got to learn to hate?

Angus Everything?

Ruth I even hate my own face because it reminds me of Albie. Have you any idea how many mirrors we have in this house? Not to mention window panes at night. Cutlery. Taps.

Angus Taps? My word.

Ruth Oh, yes. Taps give a particularly unflattering reflection, all pop-eyed and dismal.

Angus I'm going back Tuesday.

Ruth Back to America?

Angus Yes.

Ruth Do you still have a job there?

Angus Just. That's why I have to go back.

Ruth No more money?

Angus No.

Ruth I'm broke too.

Angus Is there a problem?

Ruth Is there a problem? The mortgage isn't being paid. The grass isn't being cut. Love. Marriage. Financial security. Everything I thought I couldn't live without I've lost already. You want the house too? Take it. You want the car? Take it. I'm drunk on loss. I'm a loss-a-holic. I don't even want to go on living here.

Angus Why don't you come away with me?

Ruth (*staring at him*) There was a time when I would have given my soul to hear you say that.

Angus Just an idea.

Ruth Sit on your porch with you, and watch the sun set?

Angus Why not?

Ruth Exactly how many bedrooms are there in this mountain hut of yours?

Angus One.

Ruth So what did you have in mind?

Angus Whatever you want, Ruth.

Ruth What if I want night after night of passionate love-making?

Angus Do you?

Ruth Could you?

Angus Maybe every other night.

Ruth smiles

Ruth Would you go away with you, if you were me?

Angus Probably not.

Ruth Don't say that. You're our explorer. No maps, no baggage, no ties. You must have got somewhere.

Angus I never wanted to get somewhere, Ruth.

Ruth So what did you want?

Angus Something beyond wanting. On the far side of wanting. A kind of freedom.

Ruth Does that mean not wanting?

Angus Yes.

Ruth Not wanting anything?

Angus Yes.

Ruth You thought we could sit side by side on your porch, not wanting anything together?

Bernard enters from the kitchen, carrying a tray of lunch

Sally follows him from the kitchen

Bernard Baked beans *au gratin*. (*He lays his instant meal on the floor*)

Sally, Angus and Ruth join him

What happened in church? Did your voice go?
Ruth You could say that. "In Paradisum. May angels lead you into
paradise." Why should he go to paradise? Let him burn. Not very
Christian, is it, wanting to burn your husband? I was in the middle of
singing it when I realized what I was thinking. I couldn't stay in the
church after that, could I?
Sally I'm not hungry.

Sally exits

Bernard pretends this is a response to his cooking

Bernard Do you think I overcooked the beans?

*The Lights fade on the group in the Steadman home, and come up on Albie,
in his chains in Africa. He speaks with many pauses, awkwardly, like a man
unused to the sound of his own voice. He is very frightened*

Albie There's a man here called Danny. One of my guards. Always
laughing, happy sort of soul. He's my friend, Danny. A few weeks back I
asked him, Danny, if I have to go, would you do it? He said he would. Do
it quickly, because he's my friend. He's had his orders now. He came to
tell me. Gun's not good, he's gone to get a good one. Do it right, he says. I
have a little time, not much. Only I'm finding it hard to concentrate. Fear
is distracting. I love you, but I don't know you. Danny has told me how it
will be. I kneel down and face the wall. He rests the muzzle of the gun
against the back of my neck. There's a little hollow there. He says he'll do
it quickly. So that's all. I'm not to struggle or scream. If I'm quiet, Danny
can do it right. How can I stop the scream? Just face the wall. Don't want
to go. Please don't make me go. I love you, but I don't know you.
(*Something now becomes clear to him. His agitation leaves him*) Of course.
Of course. (*He holds out his arms*) Take it. Take it.

Black-out

A newscaster's voice is heard

Newscaster There's continuing confusion over the state of British hostage
Dr Albert Steadman. Reports reaching Khartoum suggest that the
Sudanese People's Freedom Militia, who have held Dr Steadman for over
ten months now, are seeking a compromise that will lead to his release.
These reports are being treated with caution, if only because the same
sources were claiming three months ago that Dr Steadman was dead.

The Lights come up on the Steadman home

*Mary sits on the ottoman. The long months of waiting have taken their toll.
She is subdued, and internally preoccupied in a way she never was before*

Ruth stands by the piano

Ruth Albie, back. Quite a shock. Albie gone: I know what that means. Forget him, don't look back, make a new life.
Mary I still have contacts in Sudan. I get my own information.
Ruth I haven't been told anything.
Mary The Foreign Office won't admit they're negotiating.
Ruth But they are?
Mary That's what I hear.
Ruth I see. (*The more Ruth takes this in, the more she is completely thrown by the news*)
Mary I thought you had a right to know.
Ruth As the previous owner.

Sally enters with a tray of tea

Mary As his wife.
Ruth Since when did that matter?

Sally pours the tea

Sally Having a good look round? Seen anything else you fancy?
Ruth All right, Sally.
Sally Does she get the house too?
Mary I'm sorry, all right?
Sally I'm sorry, not all right. All right?
Ruth Sally!
Sally Oh, am I being bad-mannered?
Ruth Yes.
Sally And uncool, and disrespectful, and totally offensive?
Ruth Yes.

Sally drops a sugar lump into Mary's tea with a splash

Sally Great!

Sally exits

Mary Hate me if you want. I can't hate you. All these months he's been away, I've felt as if you're the only person who understands.
Ruth When are they going to release him?
Mary There aren't any dates. It could be a few days, it could be a few weeks.
Ruth A few days. A few weeks.
Mary I knew he'd come back. When I wake up I say, "It's today he's coming back." Then about noon I say, "Not today, tomorrow." And that's how it will be. One day I'll say, "He's coming back today." And he will.
Ruth I hope you're right. And what happens then?
Mary Well. He has to go somewhere, for a start.
Ruth Somewhere? Oh, I see. Your place or mine? Oh, I think yours, don't you? You were holding the parcel when the music stopped.

Mary I have a small flat in Hackney. If he goes back there with me . . . You can imagine what the press could make of it.

Ruth Are you saying he should come back here?

Mary Just for a few days.

Ruth And then what? I put him in a taxi and send him round to this small flat in Hackney?

Mary I'm just trying to think what's best for him.

Ruth I may not even be here. I've been offered a job, in Ludlow. In six weeks' time I'll be gone.

Mary Are you selling this place?

Ruth I wish I could, but it's in both our names. I'm going to try to rent it. Are you interested?

Mary Me?

Ruth I'm not serious. Albie here again. Right here in this room, leaning against my piano, waving his arms about. I was doing so well. Does it have to happen all over again? Not very dignified, is it? Being left twice by the same man.

Mary Just for a few days. Just an arrangement.

Ruth Like marriage. Just an arrangement. All right, then, if I'm still here.

Mary prepares to leave

Mary Is it all right if we keep in contact? Directly, I mean?

Ruth Yes. It's all right.

Mary I know that Sally——

Ruth I won't let her bite you.

Mary And it is good news, isn't it? For everyone.

Ruth I wish I knew.

There are the sounds of an airliner in mid-flight

Cross-fade to a plane and cloud effect

> *Albie Steadman is in a plane on his way home, accompanied by Andrew Rainer*

Albie wears a borrowed overcoat

A newscaster's voice is heard as soon as the scene is established

Newcaster British hostage Dr Albert Steadman was released in the early hours of yesterday morning, and is now on his way home. In the end, the release came unexpectedly, and there seems to have been some confusion before Dr Steadman was identified. Doctors who have examined him says he is physically healthy, but extremely tired.

Albie seems unaware of his surroundings

Rainer Do you find you've acquired a taste for solitude?

Albie Yes.

Rainer I envy you that. May I give you a small piece of advice?

Albie Yes.

Rainer Don't make any major decisions for a while. There's a well-known pattern experienced by prisoners when they're let out, called Post-Release Trauma. The shock of freedom. People do some very funny things.

Albie says nothing

I'm only talking about the first few weeks, until you're settled back into— what shall we call it?—the old routine? Back in captivity, so to speak. (*He smiles to himself, pleased by this irony*)

Albie remains silent

Be prepared for a bit of a song and dance at Heathrow. The return of the hero, and so forth. Don't feel under any obligation to speak to the press. We have a long tradition of strong silent heroes.

Albie now speaks out of his own thoughts. He has not been listening to Rainer

Albie What was the price?
Rainer The price? Of your freedom?
Albie Yes.
Rainer There was no price. How could there be? We don't do deals with terrorists.
Albie Nothing?
Rainer That does sound grudging, doesn't it? I don't mean to say you're worth nothing. I think you'll find there'll be quite a cheering crowd at the airport.
Albie Oh, I don't care about that. I just want to know the price.
Rainer I suppose it's a hobby, like train-spotting. "Let's go to Heathrow and cheer somebody." Your family will be there, of course. And Dr Hanlon, no doubt, who has campaigned so tirelessly for your release. Tiresomely, one might almost say.
Albie She usually gets what she wants.
Rainer A dangerous habit.
Albie You know, don't you?
Rainer Do you want me to know?
Albie I do feel an urge to confess something to somebody.
Rainer Post-Release Trauma. Repress it resolutely. Though to give her her due, she did create a climate in which it seemed churlish to abandon you to your fate.
Albie Please tell me.
Rainer Almost home now. Jeffreys would have been pleased.
Albie Please tell me.
Rainer It means nothing, you know. Just one of our little arrangements.
Albie Please tell me.

Rainer reflects on how much, if anything, to reveal. He decides Albie deserves to know

Rainer Does it really matter so much? A very short story, then. Once upon a time, there was an arms dealer in Tripoli, who sold guns, for cash in advance. These guns were obtained from Czechoslovakia, in exchange for oil. Then came the revolutions in Eastern Europe, and the arrangement was terminated, leaving one small consignment of spare parts, paid for but not delivered, eternally suspended in what one might call the new ideological vacuum. I understand the small consignment of spare parts has found its way, from Czechoslovakia, via Tripoli, to its rightful owners.

Albie finds this amusing

Albie A small consignment of spare parts.

An aircraft announcement tells them to prepare for landing

Rainer Welcome home, Dr Albert Russell Steadman. Wherever that may be.

The clouds fade

The plane has now landed

Albie rises and walks into a barrage of noise and light, over which booms the Newscaster's voice

   Ruth and Sally are there to greet him

   At the same time we see Mary Hanlon, alone in her office, listening to the same newscast on a transistor radio

Newscaster Albert Steadman came home today, after his year-long ordeal. He was met at Heathrow by his wife and daughter, and a cheering crowd of well-wishers.

Mary Welcome home, my love.

More and more flashes as Albie and Ruth attempt an awkward kiss for the photographers

Newscaster Dr Steadman pleaded exhaustion, and did not speak to the waiting press. But a smile and a kiss for his wife said it all. He's home safe.

The noise and the flashbulbs depart

   Rainer exits

The Lights cross-fade to the Steadman home. The walls of the Steadman home close in around the family

Sally helps Albie off with his coat

Albie does not speak

   Ruth leads Albie off to bed

Left alone, Sally hugs the coat. She finds a piece of paper in one pocket. She takes it out and opens it up: it is a map of the house, a minutely detailed ground plan of both floors. She stares at it in amazement. She compares it with the room around her

   Ruth enters

Ruth What's that?

Sally It's a map of the house. It's terrifically detailed. Look. "Hole in rug. Framed photograph of Sally with bobble hat."

Ruth Albie never notices anything. Where did he get all this from?

Sally Maybe he dreamed it. Did you leave a light on?

Ruth The landing light's on. Why?

Sally In case he wakes up in the middle of the night and thinks he's back in his prison. Where did you put him?

Ruth I didn't put him, he just went.

Sally Not your bedroom, Mum?

Ruth Yes.

Sally Where will you sleep?

Ruth I don't know.

Sally All your things are in there. You'll just have to creep into bed beside him, won't you?

Ruth I can't, can I?

Sally He'll wake up in the middle of the night and think he's back in his marriage.

Ruth Oh, Sally.

They burst into laughter together

You know the only words he's said to me so far? "Leave me alone, please."

Sally When did he say that?

Ruth Just now. Upstairs. Not in a nasty way.

Sally How do you say, "Leave me alone, please" in a nice way? (*She tries it, with a simpering smile*) "Leave me alone, please."

Ruth tries to demonstrate

Ruth It was more like, "Leave me alone, please."

Sally (*offering another version*) "Leave me alone. Please!"

Into this ridiculous exchange walks Albie, still fully dressed

As they became aware of him, they fall silent, and turn to look at him

Albie seems unaware of them

Albie I like walls. Walls are good.

Ruth Albie?

Albie (*not seeming to hear her*) Danny's outside, by the fire, with the others, drinking and laughing. I'm by the wall, waiting to die.

Sally You don't know where you are, do you?

Albie He forgot, you know.

Sally Who did?

Albie Danny.

Sally Dad?

He seems not to hear

Albie Names of the Seven Sisters?

Ruth and Sally are bewildered

White cliffs. Over there. You'd think they'd be called Lizzie, or Susie, or Harriet, but they're not. Haven Brow. Rough Brow. Short Brow. And?

Ruth Brass Point.

Albie Things to talk about, Ruth. Later, all right?

Ruth Flat Hill.

Albie Flat Hill. And? And? And?

Ruth Went Hill . . .

Albie Six. That's six. And? And? There's seven. Hence the name, the Seven Sisters. And?

Ruth I can't remember.

Sally Baily's Hill.

Albie Baily's Hill! Put it on the map. Everything goes on the map. Every time you remember something, you put it on the map, and then, one day, it's all there, and you never forget again.

Ruth Albie. Go to bed.

Albie Am I home?

Ruth You're home.

Albie Sally?

Sally Yes, Dad?

Albie What's the matter, darling?

Sally You, Dad.

Albie I'm all right. (*He takes up a glass from the sideboard and clinks it, as if to call for silence*) It's very gratifying to see so many familiar faces here this evening. I thought, rather than make a speech, I'd tell you a story.

Sally Where is he now?

Albie Suppose, just suppose, that we live in a blank world. That where we're born and who we marry and how we die is all accident.

Ruth I think he's at his farewell dinner.

Albie Just suppose that we imagine a shape to our lives, and to ourselves, but all the time, there's nothing. Then suppose a man, call him Albie, to whom certain things happen, no matter what, but the effect is that the willed world, the imagined world, cracks apart, and there on the far side he sees the blank. What happens to him now? Where is he now? No windows, no doors, no walls. Who is he now? He doesn't know. Call him. Albie! He doesn't know his name. He could be anyone, or anything. Call him whatever name you like. Fido. Here, Fido, good boy, come here! He'll come. Face the wall! He'll face the wall, even though there isn't a wall any more. You want him to die for his country? He's learned that trick in Africa. (*He lies on the ground, in the position in which he expected to be shot*) Die, boy, die! (*He jerks, as if he has been shot, and lies there, playing dead*)

Sally runs to him, deeply shocked, and takes him in her arms

Sally It's all right, Dad. In the end, you didn't die.

Albie Do you know why not?

Sally Why not?

Albie Because the man who was ordered to shoot me went to get a gun that

worked, and he met some friends, and they had a drink, and another
drink, and another drink, and he fell asleep, and he forgot. My death. A
moment of some significance in my life, and he forgot.

Sally holds him close

Sally You're my jewel and my treasure.
Albie My jewel and my treasure.
Sally That's what you always used to say to me.
Albie There's something I have to tell you.
Sally I know, Dad.
Albie I never wanted to hurt you, sweetheart. You do believe that, don't
you?
Sally No, Dad. I think you just wanted something else much, much more.

This hurts Albie so much he flinches

Ruth No, Sally. No. It's too soon.
Sally It's all right. I'm not being beastly. I'm just the same, anyway.
Albie What am I to do Sally? You tell me.

Sally doesn't know what to say

Do you want me to go?
Sally You went a year ago, Dad. (*She sees how he is suffering, and tries to
make it all right for him*) It's all right. It happens all the time. You're not
the only one. That part of our lives is over, that's all. You're back. We sell
the house. We all start a new life. All the caterpillars get to be butterflies.

Albie hears this with astonishment

Albie Sell the house? You can't sell this house. You love this house. You
can't sell the house! Something has to stay the same, for God's sake!

Albie exits in distress

Sally Sorry, Mum.

Sally holds her mother close, and they cry together

Black-out

Albie enters in the blackness and curls up on the trolley

*Mary Hanlon enters the warehouse of her charity organisation with a torch.
She is aware that somebody is there, but does not know who. She flashes the
beam of the torch around*

Mary Smithy? Is that you?

*The beam falls on Albie, curled up on the trolley. Mary stands stock still,
staring at him. Then she drops the torch and runs into his arms, and holds him
tight, and covers him with kisses*

They part, and look at each other

How are you?

Albie Hard to say.

Mary (*seeing how tired and confused Albie is*) How did you live through it? Day after day after day, all alone.

Albie I made maps. Ruth wants to sell the house. What do you think of that?

Mary She told me.

Albie Everyone knows but me.

Mary Do you need somewhere to stay?

Albie I suppose I do.

Mary You can use my place if you want.

Albie Your place?

Mary My flat. It's not very big, I know.

Albie But I don't know your flat.

Mary Yes, you do. You've been there, once. We had a bottle of Australian wine, that you called Château Sheila.

Albie Yes. I remember.

Mary And the patchwork quilt, made of stars? You said we were flying in the sky.

Albie Did I say that?

Mary Anyway, use it if you need it.

Albie I don't know.

Mary Don't you? All right.

Albie So many things I can't do.

Mary Just tell me if there's anything you want me to do. Or not do.

Albie You're a good woman, Mary.

Mary It's not exactly goodness, Russell.

Albie I should be heading back.

Mary I know it's been a long time. But nothing's changed for me. I just want you to know.

Albie Lucky you.

Mary I blame myself for what happened.

Albie starts to leave

Mary has managed so far not to speak directly of all that she is feeling. But now, seeing him about to leave, she can't stop herself

You've gone already, haven't you? So quickly.

Albie I'm sorry.

Mary Yes. Well, then. Back to work.

The introduction to "Laudate Dominum" begins

Albie It's not you, Mary.

Mary It's all right. It's happened before.

Albie It's me.

Mary No more, Russell. Please.

Albie I'm not Russell. I'm just Albie. (*He goes to the door, and then turns back*) They tell me I owe you my freedom. What can I say? Thank you.

Albie exits

The musical introduction ends

> *The Lights come up on Ruth, and she starts to sing Mozart's "Laudate Dominum".*

Ruth (*singing*) "Laudate . . ."

Mary Hanlon crosses to the position in which she made her first speech

As Ruth's singing gains in confidence and power, Mary looks up, and draws a long breath, and repeats the end of her speech for volunteers: a poignant reassertion of the faith that sustained her once, and now must sustain her again

Mary Are you leading the life you want to lead? When it's over, will you look back and say, That wasn't what I meant to do at all? (*For a moment, she falters*) That wasn't what I meant to do at all. (*She recovers*) For six years now I've known the greatest freedom life has to offer. If I die tomorrow, I'll be able to say, I lived the life I wanted to live. Will you?

Ruth's singing reaches its powerful conclusion, and the Lights fade on both Ruth and Mary

The Lights come up on the Steadman home

> *Bernard is playing the piano and singing a song, "Leaning", in a comic rustic accent*

> *Albie sits on the ottoman, listening, and waiting*

Bernard   "Had a lurcher once, better than a gal;
Poacher? Well, a bit, but he was a pal.
Now there's just a mound
Underneath the ellum,
Reckon folks would laugh at oi
If I was to tell 'em
Why I'm
Leanin' on the gate beside the pond that
Lies beside the hedge where my old dog
Would play,
It's just a-cos from there I see the
Sunlight glintin' through the tree upon
The grave where 'e do lie
Sleepin', sleepin',
Goodbye is hard to say——"

Bernard pauses as:

> *Ruth enters*

Albie I hate you, Bernard. I want to smash your fingers in the bloody piano.

Bernard runs his fingers down the keyboard, and picks up the end of his song

Bernard   "That's why
I'm leanin' on the gate beside the pond

That lies beside the side of farmer's
Stacks of new-mown hay,
And at the gleanin', he'll find me
Leanin'
All day." (*He looks up as he finishes*)

Albie starts to leave the room

Bernard I wish someone would kidnap me. Instant significance. Instant purpose in life. And really, very little on the debit side. Though I expect they beat you a little from time to time?
Albie Actually, no.
Bernard No beatings? I don't know how you could tear yourself away.

Albie turns back and comes over to Bernard

Albie Bernard, you do know what's been going on between Ruth and me?
Bernard Certainly not. *Terra incognita.*
Ruth You have the general idea.
Bernard It's the details that do the damage. Keep it fuzzy, that's the trick.
Albie I always thought it was Angus, but it's Bernard, isn't it? Bernard, and the sweet anaesthetic of childhood.
Ruth What do you mean?
Albie It doesn't matter. I'll go and pack.

Albie exits

Bernard He has a wobbly look about him, Ruth.
Ruth Haven't we all?
Bernard All except you. A year ago you couldn't live without him. Now, you send him packing.
Ruth Albie doesn't know how to pack.
Bernard Don't tell me you used to do it for him.
Ruth I just couldn't bear to watch.
Bernard You don't do my packing for me.
Ruth You never go away.
Bernard All you have to do is say the word.

Bernard picks out the tune of "Keep the Home Fires Burning" on the piano

Roo. May I make you a confession?
Ruth "I've turned the dark cloud inside out."
Bernard "Till the boys come home."
Ruth He is leaving again.
Bernard Is he?

Albie enters with an overnight bag

Albie Goodbye, Bernard.
Bernard (*standing*) You're off, are you, Albie?
Albie No. You are.
Bernard Am I? Where am I going?

Albie I don't really care. I'd like a few minutes with Ruth.

Bernard Ah. Would you? I'm to go, am I? Roo? (*He turns to Ruth*)

Ruth No. You're to stay.

Bernard Righto. (*He goes and sits on the piano stool, with his back to Albie and Ruth, as if to offer them some privacy*)

Albie You protect him.

Ruth We protect each other.

Albie You, and Bernard, and the piano, and those bloody old songs.

Ruth It's just how we grew up, Albie.

Albie Yes, I know. But I wasn't part of it, was I? Still, water under the bridge.

Ruth Where are you going now?

Albie The Blakes, I thought.

Ruth Have you phoned them?

Albie Not yet.

Ruth What are you taking?

Albie Shirts. Socks. The usual things. Why Ludlow?

Ruth Because that's where I've been offered a post. I'm lucky to get it.

Albie Will Bernard go with you?

Ruth If he wants to.

Albie I can't find my map. I spent weeks on that map. (*Without waiting for an answer, he turns on Ruth*) Could I just say goodbye without him hovering like a vulture over a dying animal?

Bernard rises and closes the piano with dignity

Bernard Chin up, Bernard. Tummy in. Best foot forward. *Tristesse oblige.*

Bernard exits

Ruth Well?

Albie goes to the fire and proceeds to build it and light it

Albie I'm cold. Don't you heat the house any more?

Ruth watches his slow deliberate preparations for the fire

Ruth How long is this goodbye going to last?

Albie This man went to Africa. (*He tells his story while busying himself at the fire, so that he does not have to watch Ruth's reaction*) Sort of an explorer, except that he didn't get very far. Because they chained him up. Then one day they told him they were going to shoot him. Dead.

Ruth Haven't I heard this story before?

Albie They gave him a pencil and paper, so that he could write a last letter. A small kindness. He didn't know what to write. He was crazy with fear. Then he wrote on the piece of paper: "I love you, but I don't know you." Then he does a funny thing. He reaches out his arms, as if he's carrying something. And he says, out loud: "Take it. Take it." (*He reaches out his arms, as he did in his prison*)

Ruth Take what?

Albie All my love. (*He drops his arms, and looks into the fire, and falls silent*)
Ruth "I love you, but I don't know you"?
Albie Yes.
Ruth It won't do, Albie.
Albie I'm not finding this easy, you know.
Ruth I'm not staying here, whatever you say.
Albie I didn't say anything.
Ruth I want to sell the house.
Albie Sell it.
Ruth I'm going to take the job in Ludlow.
Albie Take it. (*He rises, and takes up his bag*)

Albie pauses by Ruth and puts an arm round her. Then he goes to the door

Ruth I took your map.

Albie comes to a stop

Albie Why?
Ruth For old times' sake, I suppose. Maps are much better than diaries. Nothing about what we wanted or didn't want. Nothing about what we said or didn't say. The world we had in common. The spaces we shared. Where we were.

Ruth goes to the deed box where she keeps her diaries, and takes out the map. She gives it to Albie, and goes and sits in front of the fire on the ottoman

It's a long time since we had a fire.

After a moment, Albie joins her on the ottoman. He sits down with his back to her. He hands her the map back. Slowly, they lean against each other, supporting each other's weight, back to back, in silence. Then Ruth's head falls back onto his shoulder, and they are very close, in the firelight

CURTAIN

FURNITURE AND PROPERTY LIST

ACT I

The living-room of the Steadman home

On stage: Piano. *On it:* framed family photographs
            Fireplace. *In it:* a dying fire. *By it:* poker and some logs
            Piano stool
            Ottoman. *On it:* Sunday newspaper and colour supplement
            Drinks cabinet. *In it:* bottles of drink including vodka and glasses. *On it:* telephone
            Easy chairs
            Desk: *In it:* Ruth's make-up, including her lipstick and a mirror. *On it:* lamp
            Sofa

Off stage: Purse **(Ruth)**
            Can of beer **(Sally)**

Personal: **Albie:** wallet. *In it:* five-pound note and a twenty-pound note

The office and warehouse of a charity organisation

On stage: Stacks of boxes
            Desk. *On it:* piles of papers, notepad and pen
            Chair

Off stage: Trolley. *On it:* boxes **(Smithy)**

Personal: **Albie:** watch (worn throughout)

The living-room of the Steadman home

Strike: Can of beer and used glasses

On stage: As before
            Red exercise book
            Deed box. *In it:* similar red exercise books

Off stage: Shoes **(Sally)**

The office and warehouse of a charity organisation

On stage: As before

Off stage: Trolley. *On it:* boxes. *In one:* a union-jack sock **(Smithy)**
            Clipboard and pen **(Mary)**
            Carton **(Albie)**
            Carton. *In it:* used Christmas cards **(Smithy)**
            Second carton. *In it:* used Christmas cards **(Smithy)**

Personal: **Smithy:** watch

A cliff top

On stage: Table cloth. *On it:* picnic things and food

The living-room of the Steadman home

Strike: Red exercise book and deed box

On stage: As before
             Luggage

Off stage: Tray. *On it:* teapot, cups and saucers **(Ruth)**

Personal: **Albie:** flight ticket

A room in a staff bungalow in Africa

On stage: Wide bed. *Over it:* mosquito net

ACT II

A television studio

On stage: Chair
             Trolley. *On it:* make-up, make-up brushes and a mirror
             Easy chairs
             TV camera
             Trolley: *On it:* bottles of alcohol and glasses

Personal: **Rainer:** piece of paper in his pocket
             June: ear-piece

The living-room of the Steadman home

Strike: Luggage and tea tray

On stage: As before

Africa

On stage: Cage
             Dust on the floor

Personal: **Albie:** chains

The Steadman home

On stage: As before

Off stage: Large bag of crisps **(Sally)**
             Tray. *On it:* plates, cutlery and serving dish **(Bernard)**

Africa

On stage: As before

Personal: **Albie:** chains

The Steadman home

Strike: Bag of crisps and lunch tray

On stage: As before

Off stage: Tray. *On it:* teapot, cups, saucers and sugar bowl. *In it:* sugar lumps
           (Sally)

On the plane

On stage: Two plane seats

Personal: **Albie:** borrowed overcoat. *In a pocket:* piece of paper. *On it:* hand-drawn
           map

The office of a charity organisation

On stage: As before
            Transistor radio

The living-room of the Steadman home

Strike: Tray and crockery

On stage: As before

The office of Mary Hanlon's charity organisation

On stage: As before
            Trolley

Off stage: Torch **(Mary)**

The living-room of the Steadman home

On stage: As before
            Fire is dead

Off stage: Overnight bag **(Albie)**

LIGHTING PLOT

Property fittings required: lamp and fire-glow in the Steadman home

Various interior and exterior settings

ACT I

To open: Black-out

Cue 1	An organ plays the introduction to the communion, *"Panis Angelicus"* *Lights up on* **Ruth Steadman**	(Page 1)
Cue 2	**Ruth** exits *Lights up on the living-room of the Steadman home, faint fire-glow*	(Page 1)
Cue 3	**Ruth** restarts the fire *Fire-glow effect increases*	(Page 3)
Cue 4	**Sally**, **Angus** and **Albie** exit *Lights fade and came up on* **Mary Hanlon**	(Page 10)
Cue 5	As **Mary**'s speech ends *Lights come up on the office and warehouse of a charity organisation*	(Page 11)
Cue 6	**Mary** exits *Cross-fade to the Steadman home*	(Page 14)
Cue 7	**Ruth** stares at him as if he has become a stranger *Cross-fade to* **Mary Hanlon**'s *office and warehouse*	(Page 18)
Cue 8	**Albie** and **Mary** kiss again *Lights come up on* **Ruth**	(Page 20)
Cue 9	When ready *Slowly fade Lights on the embracing couple and* **Ruth** *to Black-out*	(Page 20)
Cue 10	The anthem finishes *Lights come up bright to represent a cliff top*	(Page 20)
Cue 11	**Angus** exits after **Ruth** *Cross-fade to the Steadman home*	(Page 22)
Cue 12	**Bernard:** "Here I am." *Cross-fade to a staff bungalow in Africa*	(Page 26)
Cue 13	**Albie** is drawn inexorably out of sight *Fade to Black-out*	(Page 26)

ACT II

To open: Bright general lighting

Cue 14	**June** exits *Cross-fade to the Steadman home*	(Page 33)
Cue 15	**Ruth** and **Bernard** exit *Cross-fade to Africa*	(Page 34)
Cue 16	**Albie:** "Get it?" *Lights fade on* **Albie**	(Page 35)
Cue 17	The organ plays the introduction to *In Paradisum*, from Fauré's Requiem *Lights come up on* **Ruth**	(Page 35)
Cue 18	**Ruth** exits *Cross-fade to the Steadman home*	(Page 35)
Cue 19	**Bernard:** "Do you think I overcooked the beans?" *Cross-fade to Africa*	(Page 39)
Cue 20	**Albie:** "Take it. Take it." *Black-out*	(Page 39)
Cue 21	**Newscaster:** ". . . Dr Steadman was dead." *Lights come up on the Steadman home*	(Page 39)
Cue 22	There are the sounds of an airliner in mid-flight *Cross-fade to plane*	(Page 41)
Cue 23	**Albie** rises *Increase lighting and bring lights up on* **Mary Hanlon's** office	(Page 43)
Cue 24	**Albie** and **Ruth** attempt an awkward kiss *Flashbulbs*	(Page 43)
Cue 25	**Newscaster:** "He's home safe." *Cut flashbulbs and cross-fade to the Steadman home*	(Page 43)
Cue 26	**Sally** holds her mother close, and they cry together *Black-out*	(Page 46)
Cue 27	The musical introduction ends *Lights come up on* **Ruth**	(Page 48)
Cue 28	**Ruth's** singing reaches its powerful conclusion *Lights fade on* **Ruth** *and* **Mary** *and come up on the Steadman home*	(Page 48)
Cue 29	**Albie** builds and lights the fire *Fire-glow*	(Page 50)

EFFECTS PLOT

ACT I

MADE AND PRINTED IN GREAT BRITAIN BY
LATIMER TREND & COMPANY LTD PLYMOUTH

MADE IN ENGLAND